SAQUON BARKLEY

CHARLIE BEATTIE

WWW.APEXEDITIONS.COM

Copyright © 2026 by Apex Editions, Mendota Heights, MN 55120. All rights reserved. No part of this book may be reproduced or utilized in any form or by any means without written permission from the publisher.

Apex is distributed by North Star Editions:
sales@northstareditions.com | 888-417-0195

Produced for Apex by Red Line Editorial.

Photographs ©: Peter Joneleit/AP Images, cover, 1; Mitchell Leff/Getty Images Sport/Getty Images, 4–5, 57; Elsa/Getty Images Sport/Getty Images, 6–7; Shutterstock Images, 8–9; Gary Newkirk/Getty Images Sport/Getty Images, 10–11; iStockphoto, 12–13; Joe Hermitt/PennLive.com/AP Images, 14–15, 16–17; Joe Robbins/Getty Images Sport/Getty Images, 18–19; Brett Carlsen/Getty Images Sport/Getty Images, 20–21, 34–35; Norm Hall/Getty Images Sport/Getty Images, 22–23; Tom Pennington/Getty Images Sport/Getty Images, 24–25, 32–33; Leon Bennett/Getty Images Sport/Getty Images, 27; Jim McIsaac/Getty Images Sport/Getty Images, 28–29; Patrick Smith/Getty Images Sport/Getty Images, 30–31, 42–43; Jonathan Bachman/Getty Images Sport/Getty Images, 36–37; Sarah Stier/Getty Images Sport/Getty Images, 38–39; David Berding/Getty Images Sport/Getty Images, 40–41; Al Bello/Getty Images Sport/Getty Images, 44–45; Chris Szagola/AP Images, 46–47; Brooke Sutton/Getty Images Sport/Getty Images, 48–49; Cooper Neill/AP Images, 50–51, 58–59; Ronald Martinez/Getty Images Sport/Getty Images, 52–53; Gregory Shamus/Getty Images Sport/Getty Images, 54–55

Library of Congress Control Number: 2024952003

ISBN
979-8-89250-721-9 (hardcover)
979-8-89250-773-8 (paperback)
979-8-89250-755-4 (ebook pdf)
979-8-89250-739-4 (hosted ebook)

Printed in the United States of America
Mankato, MN
082025

NOTE TO PARENTS AND EDUCATORS

Apex books are designed to build literacy skills in striving readers. Exciting, high-interest content attracts and holds readers' attention. The text is carefully

TABLE OF CONTENTS

CHAPTER 1
QUITE A LEAP 4

CHAPTER 2
PENNSYLVANIA PROUD 8

CHAPTER 3
COLLEGE STAR 16

IN THE SPOTLIGHT
RUN FOR THE ROSES 26

CHAPTER 4
A GIANT START 28

CHAPTER 5
A BIG MOVE 38

CHAPTER 6
SOARING EAGLE 48

IN THE SPOTLIGHT
ALL-TIME GREAT 56

TIMELINE • 58
COMPREHENSION QUESTIONS • 60
GLOSSARY • 62
TO LEARN MORE • 63
ABOUT THE AUTHOR • 63
INDEX • 64

CHAPTER 1

QUITE A LEAP

Saquon Barkley caught a pass near the sideline. A Jacksonville Jaguars defender met him. Barkley juked to his right. Then he spun around another defender. Barkley was now facing the wrong direction. And another Jaguar was closing in from behind.

Saquon Barkley dodges a defender during a 2024 game against the Jacksonville Jaguars.

Barkley's reverse hurdle quickly went viral. People watched it millions of times online.

What Barkley did next was magical. The Philadelphia Eagles' star running back didn't turn around. Instead, he leaped backward and spread his legs wide. Barkley hurdled the defender, who dived right under him. Eagles coach Nick Sirianni called it the best play he had ever seen.

IT'S IN THE GAME

Electronic Arts (EA) puts out the *Madden NFL* video game before each season. Usually, the company doesn't make changes until the next year's game. Then came Barkley's "spin hurdle." A few weeks later, EA added the move to the game.

CHAPTER 2

PENNSYLVANIA PROUD

Saquon Barkley was born on February 9, 1997, in the Bronx, New York. His family moved to Pennsylvania in 2001. They lived in many spots. Things weren't always easy for his family. Saquon had no home for nearly a year.

One of the places Saquon Barkley's family lived after moving to Pennsylvania was Allentown.

In 2005, Saquon's family moved to Coplay, Pennsylvania. Coplay is 10 minutes from Lehigh University. For many years, the Philadelphia Eagles held their summer training camp at the school. Many kids watched the Eagles practice. Saquon was one of them. He fell in love with football.

BOXING FAMILY

Saquon Barkley comes from a family of boxers. His father, Alibay, taught a young Saquon how to box. Saquon's uncle Iran was a three-time world champion in the 1980s and 1990s.

Saquon's uncle Iran became a boxing world champion in three different weight classes.

In high school, Saquon started spending more time in the weight room.

As a kid, Saquon wasn't big. He didn't think he would play football past high school. Even so, he was a great athlete. In his sophomore year, Saquon made an incredible catch on a Hail Mary pass. College teams started to take notice of his skills. Saquon soon agreed to a scholarship offer from Rutgers University.

THREE-SPORT STAR
Saquon also played basketball and ran track in high school. On the track, he showed off his blazing speed. He ran the 100 meters in 10.9 seconds. That set a school record.

13

Pennsylvania State University head coach James Franklin loved watching Saquon play. He hoped the running back would play for Penn State instead. At first, Saquon didn't want to. He had given his word to Rutgers. But Franklin wouldn't give up. He convinced Saquon to go to Penn State.

SUPER BOWL WINNERS

Saquon's high school has a proud football tradition. Linebacker Matt Millen and offensive lineman Dan Koppen both went there. Millen won the Super Bowl four times in the 1980s and early 1990s. Koppen won it twice in the 2000s.

Saquon Barkley (center) visits a Penn State football practice in 2014.

CHAPTER 3

COLLEGE STAR

In college, Saquon Barkley grew bigger and stronger. But he kept his speed and agility. In his second game with the Penn State Nittany Lions, he ran for 115 yards. The next month, he ran for 194 yards against No. 1 Ohio State.

Saquon Barkley (26) leaps over defenders during a 2015 game for Penn State.

Barkley scored two touchdowns in the 2016 Big Ten Conference Championship Game.

Barkley finished the 2015 season with 1,076 rushing yards. That set a Penn State record for freshmen. Barkley outdid himself the next year. He ran for more than 1,400 yards. He also led the Big Ten Conference with 22 total touchdowns. Barkley was named the conference's Offensive Player of the Year that season.

SAQUADS

Barkley dedicated himself to the weight room. In 2017, he lifted 405 pounds (184 kg). A video of him went viral. Fans watched it millions of times. His leg strength earned him the nickname "SaQuads."

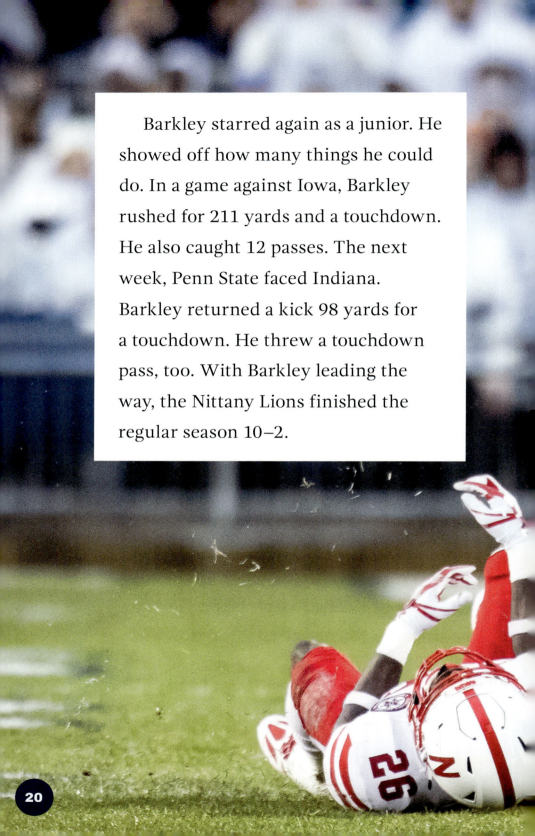

Barkley starred again as a junior. He showed off how many things he could do. In a game against Iowa, Barkley rushed for 211 yards and a touchdown. He also caught 12 passes. The next week, Penn State faced Indiana. Barkley returned a kick 98 yards for a touchdown. He threw a touchdown pass, too. With Barkley leading the way, the Nittany Lions finished the regular season 10–2.

In 2017, Barkley led the Big Ten again with 21 total touchdowns.

The Nittany Lions played Washington in the 2017 Fiesta Bowl. In the second quarter, Barkley took a handoff at his own 8-yard line. He exploded through the line. Then he took off down the sideline. He scored a 92-yard touchdown. Penn State won 35–28.

RECORD BREAKER

Barkley set many records at Penn State. For example, he racked up 358 total yards in a game. No Nittany Lion had ever done that. Barkley also set a career record by scoring 43 rushing touchdowns.

Barkley leaps into the end zone for his 92-yard touchdown in the 2017 Fiesta Bowl.

Barkley takes a picture with NFL commissioner Roger Goodell after being drafted by the New York Giants in 2018.

Barkley earned All-America honors as a junior. He decided he was ready for the next level. So, Barkley skipped his senior season. He entered the NFL Draft. The New York Giants selected Barkley second overall. No running back had been picked that high in 12 years.

SAQUON BARKLEY DAY
Coplay, Pennsylvania, celebrated Barkley in 2018. The state declared March 14 Saquon Barkley Day. That month, he was honored with a parade through his hometown.

IN THE SPOTLIGHT

RUN FOR THE ROSES

One of Saquon Barkley's best games took place on one of college football's biggest stages. Penn State faced USC in the Rose Bowl on January 2, 2017. Early in the second quarter, Barkley broke a 24-yard touchdown run. In the third, Barkley weaved through the defense. He dodged nearly every defender for a 79-yard score. Later, he caught a touchdown pass.

Barkley finished with 306 total yards. Penn State ended up losing the thrilling game. But Barkley's performance was what many fans remembered.

BARKLEY HAD 194 RUSHING YARDS, 55 RECEIVING YARDS, AND 57 RETURN YARDS IN THE 2017 ROSE BOWL.

CHAPTER 4

A GIANT START

Barkley's NFL career got off to a great start. He played the Jacksonville Jaguars in his first game. In the fourth quarter, Barkley broke loose for a 68-yard score. It was his first NFL touchdown.

Barkley takes a handoff during his first NFL game.

In Week 14 of the 2018 season, Barkley racked up a season-high 170 rushing yards.

Barkley continued to succeed throughout his rookie season. He finished with 1,307 rushing yards and 15 total touchdowns. Barkley was named the Offensive Rookie of the Year. New York finished just 5–11. But Giants fans were thrilled to have a new star.

NEW YORK HISTORY

The New York Giants played their first season in 1925. For 93 years, no Giants running back had topped 1,000 yards in his first season. In 2018, Barkley became the first.

Barkley wasn't just a new star player. He quickly developed into a team leader, too. The Giants named him a captain before his second season. In 2019, Barkley was one of seven captains on the team.

A SPECIAL HONOR

NFL teams pick captains in different ways. The Giants vote for their captains. Teams rarely name a second-year player as a captain. But Barkley earned the honor. He was also the first running back to become a captain of the Giants.

Team captains wear patches with the letter C on their jerseys.

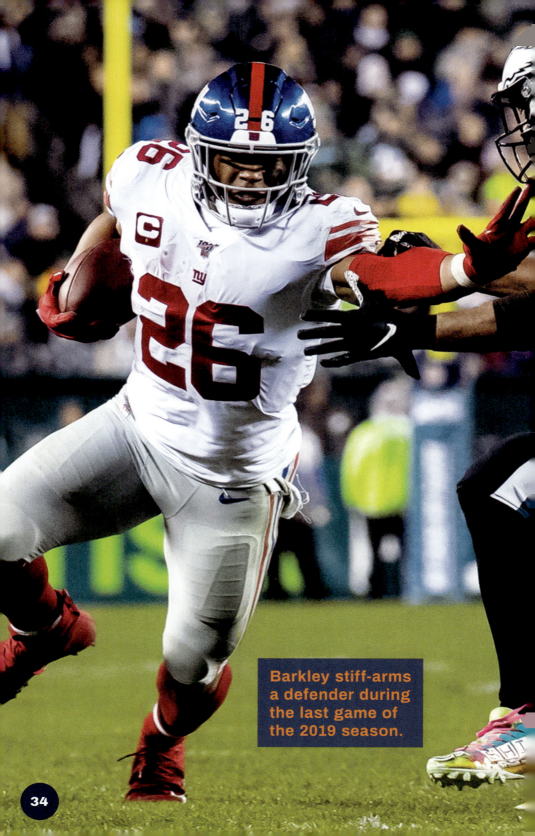

Barkley stiff-arms a defender during the last game of the 2019 season.

The Giants struggled again in 2019. But Barkley still shined. He finished with 1,003 rushing yards even though he missed three games. He also caught 52 passes. And he scored eight touchdowns.

PEACE

Barkley ended the 2019 season in style. The Giants faced the Philadelphia Eagles. In the third quarter, Barkley burst through the line. Then he sped past most of the defenders. As Barkley passed the last one, he held up a peace sign. He cruised into the end zone for a 68-yard touchdown.

35

Barkley hoped for a big year in 2020. But during his second game, he hurt his knee. He didn't play again until the 2021 season. That year, Barkley struggled to produce. He ran for only 537 yards in 13 games. However, things would soon turn around for Barkley and the Giants.

HOMETOWN HERO

In 2021, Barkley's high school retired his No. 21 jersey. That means the number will never be worn by another player. Barkley was just the third player in the school's history to have his number retired.

In Week 4 of the 2021 season, Barkley scored the game-winning touchdown in overtime to beat the New Orleans Saints.

CHAPTER 5

A BIG MOVE

Barkley came back strong in 2022. He ran for 1,312 yards and 10 touchdowns. He caught 57 passes, too. After the season, Barkley was named to the Pro Bowl. It was the second time he had earned that honor.

Barkley leaps for a touchdown during a 2022 game against the Baltimore Ravens.

The Giants finished 9–7–1 in 2022. That was good enough to make the playoffs. In the first round, New York took on the Minnesota Vikings. Barkley scored two touchdowns in his first NFL playoff game. His second was the game-winner. The Giants won 31–24.

COLLEGE GRADUATE

Barkley returned to Penn State in the spring of 2022. He finished his college degree in communications. It was a special day. Barkley became the first member of his family to graduate from college.

Barkley scores on a 28-yard run for his first NFL playoff touchdown.

Giants fans were excited for 2023. And Barkley performed well. He rushed for 962 yards and scored 10 total touchdowns. But the team couldn't build on the previous season's success. The Giants finished just 6–11. Barkley felt frustrated. He wanted to make the playoffs again.

FAMILY MAN

Barkley started dating his partner, Anna Congdon, in 2017 at Penn State. They started a family together. Their daughter, Jada, was born in 2018. Their son, Saquon Jr., was born in 2022.

In 2023, Barkley scored two of his ten touchdowns in Week 11 against the Washington Commanders.

Barkley's last touchdown as a Giant came against the Eagles on January 7, 2024.

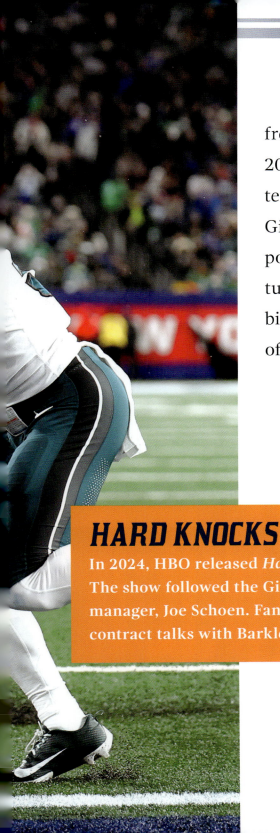

Barkley became a free agent after the 2023 season. Many NFL teams wanted him. The Giants also wanted the popular star back. It turned into one of the biggest stories of the offseason.

HARD KNOCKS

In 2024, HBO released *Hard Knocks: Offseason*. The show followed the Giants' general manager, Joe Schoen. Fans saw the team's contract talks with Barkley.

Giants fans hoped Barkley would stay. So did team owner John Mara. But the Philadelphia Eagles offered Barkley a great contract. And the Giants chose not to match the deal. Barkley felt disappointed that the Giants didn't try harder to keep him.

Even so, Barkley looked forward to the new opportunity. For the second time in his life, he was leaving New York for Pennsylvania. He was going to play for the team he'd cheered for growing up.

CHAPTER 6

SOARING EAGLE

Barkley joined a strong team in Philadelphia. The Eagles had reached the Super Bowl after the 2022 season. And Barkley made them even better. He scored three touchdowns in his first game with the team. No Eagles player had done that in their debut in 20 years.

Barkley carries the ball downfield during a 2024 game.

In Week 7, the Eagles faced the Giants on the road. Barkley took the big day in stride. He ripped up his old team for 176 rushing yards and a touchdown. Giants fans booed him early in the game. Later, they cheered him on.

SPEED DEMON

The NFL tracks how fast players move on the field. In Week 3 of the 2024 season, Barkley showed off his amazing speed. On one run against the New Orleans Saints, he ran 21.7 miles per hour (34.9 km/h).

Philadelphia's offensive line excelled at creating gaps in the defense. Barkley (26) used those gaps to make big runs.

Barkley leaves Los Angeles Rams defenders in the dust during a 70-yard touchdown run in 2024.

After the Giants game, Barkley took off. He ran for more than 100 yards in six of his next seven games. The Eagles won them all.

Barkley finished the 2024 regular season with a whopping 2,005 rushing yards. That led the NFL. He won Offensive Player of the Year. With Barkley leading the way, the Eagles easily made the playoffs.

BIG GAINS

Barkley's best game came in Week 12 against the Los Angeles Rams. He had one 70-yard touchdown run and one 72-yard score. He finished with a team record 255 yards.

The Eagles made it all the way to the Super Bowl. They faced the defending champions, the Kansas City Chiefs. The Eagles crushed Kansas City 40–22. Barkley was a Super Bowl champion!

Barkley also made more history in the big game. He finished with 2,504 rushing yards in the regular season and playoffs. That was the most by any player in NFL history.

Barkley holds the Vince Lombardi Trophy after becoming a Super Bowl champion.

IN THE SPOTLIGHT

ALL-TIME GREAT

On December 29, 2024, the Philadelphia Eagles faced the Dallas Cowboys. Saquon Barkley already had 1,838 rushing yards that season. By the fourth quarter, he had 1,953. The Eagles went to Barkley on five straight plays. On the fifth play, he burst through the defense for a 23-yard gain. That gave Barkley 2,005 yards. He became just the ninth player ever to top 2,000 rushing yards in a season. Eagles fans couldn't wait to see more from their superstar running back.

IN 2024, BARKLEY AVERAGED 125.3 RUSHING YARDS PER GAME. THAT LED THE LEAGUE.

TIMELINE

1997 — Saquon Barkley is born in the Bronx, New York, on February 9.

2005 — Saquon Barkley and his family move to Coplay, Pennsylvania.

2015 — Barkley begins attending Pennsylvania State University.

2017 — Barkley is named an All-American after leading Penn State to an 11–2 season.

2018 — The New York Giants select Barkley second overall in the NFL Draft.

2019 — **2022** — **2024** — **2024** — **2025**

2022: Barkley lifts the Giants to their first playoff appearance since 2016.

2024: On December 29, Barkley becomes the ninth NFL player ever to top 2,000 rushing yards in a season.

2019: On February 2, Barkley is named the 2018 Offensive Rookie of the Year.

2024: On March 13, Barkley signs with the Philadelphia Eagles.

2025: On February 9, Barkley wins his first Super Bowl championship.

59

COMPREHENSION QUESTIONS

Write your answers on a separate piece of paper.

1. Write a paragraph that explains the main ideas of Chapter 4.

2. What are some of Saquon Barkley's best skills as a football player?

3. How many yards did Saquon Barkley run for in the 2024 regular season?
    - A. 1,003
    - B. 1,307
    - C. 2,005

4. Why did Barkley skip his senior year of college?
    - A. He was ready to play in the NFL after his junior year.
    - B. He planned on switching to Rutgers.
    - C. He knew he never wanted to graduate from college.

5. What does **hurdled** mean in this book?

   *Instead, he leaped backward and spread his legs wide. Barkley **hurdled** the defender, who dived right under him.*

   A. dived under
   B. jumped over
   C. smashed into

6. What does **dedicated** mean in this book?

   *Barkley **dedicated** himself to the weight room. In 2017, he lifted 405 pounds (184 kg).*

   A. tried hard to improve something
   B. stopped trying to do something
   C. got hurt while lifting weights

Answer key on page 64.

GLOSSARY

agility
Being able to move quickly and easily.

conference
A group of teams that make up part of a sports league.

contract
A written agreement that keeps a player with a team for a certain amount of time.

draft
A system that lets teams select new players coming into the league.

free agent
A professional athlete who doesn't have a contract with a team and is free to sign with any team.

general manager
The person in a team's front office who drafts and signs new players.

playoffs
A set of games played after the regular season to decide which team is the champion.

rookie
An athlete in his or her first year as a professional player.

scholarship
Money given to someone to help pay for college.

tradition
A history of doing something well over a period of many years.

TO LEARN MORE

BOOKS

Anderson, Josh. *New York Giants*. The Child's World, 2023.

Lowe, Alexander. *G.O.A.T. Football Running Backs*. Lerner Publications, 2023.

Scheff, Matt. *Philadelphia Eagles*. Apex Editions, 2025.

ONLINE RESOURCES

Visit **www.apexeditions.com** to find links and resources related to this title.

ABOUT THE AUTHOR

Charlie Beattie is a writer and former sportscaster. Originally from St. Paul, Minnesota, he now lives in Charleston, South Carolina, with his wife and son.

INDEX

All-America honors, 25

Barkley, Alibay, 10
Barkley, Iran, 10
Big Ten Conference, 19
Bronx, New York, 9

Congdon, Anna, 42
Coplay, Pennsylvania, 10, 25

Fiesta Bowl, 22

Hard Knocks: Offseason, 45
high school, 13–14, 36

Koppen, Dan, 14

Lehigh University, 10

Madden NFL, 7
Millen, Matt, 14

New York Giants, 25, 31–32, 35–36, 40, 42, 45–46, 50, 53
NFL Draft, 25

Pennsylvania State University, 14, 16, 19–20, 22, 26, 40, 42
Philadelphia Eagles, 7, 10, 35, 46, 48, 50, 53–54, 56
playoffs, 40, 42, 53–54
Pro Bowl, 38

Rose Bowl, 26
Rutgers University, 13–14

Schoen, Joe, 45
Sirianni, Nick, 7
Super Bowl, 14, 48, 54

team captains, 32

ANSWER KEY:
1. Answers will vary; 2. Answers will vary; 3. C; 4. A; 5. B; 6. A